MEASURING AND COMPARING

How Tall Is Tall?
Comparing Structures

Vic Parker

Heinemann
LIBRARY

Chicago, Illinois

www.heinemannraintree.com
Visit our website to find out
more information about
Heinemann-Raintree books.

To order:
☏ Phone 888-454-2279
🖳 Visit www.heinemannraintree.com
to browse our catalog and order online.

Edited by Nancy Dickmann, Rebecca Rissman, and Sian Smith
Designed by Victoria Allen
Picture research by Hannah Taylor
Original illustrations © Capstone Global Library Ltd
Original illustrations by Victoria Allen
Production by Victoria Fitzgerald
Originated by Dot Gradations Ltd
Printed and bound in China by South China Printing
 Company Ltd

14 13 12 11 10
10 9 8 7 6 5 4 3 2 1

Library of Congress Cataloging-in-Publication Data
Parker, Victoria.
 How tall is tall?:comparing structures / Vic Parker.
  p. cm.—(Measuring and comparing)
 Includes bibliographical references and index.
 ISBN 978-1-4329-3955-7 (hc)—ISBN 978-1-4329-3963-2
(pb) 1. Tall buildings—Juvenile literature. 2. Skyscrapers—
Juvenile literature. 3. Weights and measures—Juvenile
literature. I. Title.
 NA6230.P375 2011
 720'.483—dc22
                                    2010000924

Acknowledgments
The author and publisher are grateful to the following for
permission to reproduce copyright material: Alamy Images pp.
10 (© vario images GmbH & Co.KG), **12** (© inga spence), **18**
(© JLImages); © Capstone Publishers pp. **4**, **8**, **26**, **27** (Karon
Dubke); Corbis p. **24** (epa/ Peter Kneffel); istockphoto p. **20** (©
Henryk Sadura); Photolibrary pp. **5**, **6** (age fotostock/
P. Narayan), **7** (Len Delessio); shutterstock pp. **14** (© BEEE),
16 (© upthebanner); Wayne Howes p. **22**.

Photographs used to create silhouettes: shutterstock, child
(© angel digital), house (© Andrii Syneok), pylon (© Fica),
London Eye (© Cihan Demirok, CIDEPIX), Golden Gate
Bridge (© Slobodan Djajic), Eiffel Tower (© Ints Vikmanis),
Willis Tower (© jamaican).

Cover photograph of the skyline from Brooklyn Heights
promenade, in New York, reproduced with permission of
Photolibrary (Steve Dunwell).

Contents

Words appearing in the text in bold, like this, are explained in the glossary.

Measuring Height

The height of something is how tall it is. To measure height you can use a ruler, wall chart, tape measure, or measuring stick. These are marked in inches (in.) and feet (ft.).

A door handle is often over 3 feet high.

There are some things we cannot reach the top of, such as buildings. To measure the height of buildings, experts use special tools that look like cameras.

This **surveyor** is measuring the height of a building.

Why Do People Build Tall Structures?

Tall buildings can be useful. This is because they can fit hundreds or even thousands of people inside, without taking up much ground. This is helpful in crowded cities.

The city of Shanghai, in China, has many tall skyscrapers.

Tall structures can be impressive and beautiful. The Statue of Liberty stands in New York Harbor, in New York. People on ships heading for the city can see the statue from a long way off.

Some people think the Statue of Liberty looks like it is welcoming people to New York.

Measure Your Height

Have you ever measured how tall you are? Compared to a younger brother or sister, you might be tall. But how tall is tall?

You can measure yourself in inches or feet.

A house with two floors is often about 24½ feet high. If you and five of your friends stood on top of each other, you would not quite reach the top of a house.

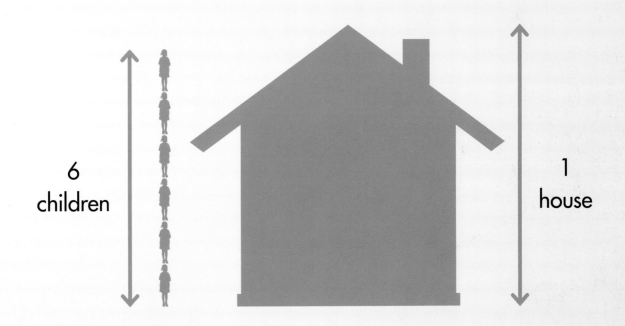

6
children

1
house

What is taller than a house? ➡

Electrical Towers

An **electrical tower** is taller than a house.
Electrical towers are made from steel. They
carry cables for **electricity** from place
to place.

Electricity is the energy
that powers equipment
such as lights, televisions,
and computers.

A regular electrical tower is about 164 feet tall. This is higher than six houses on top of each other.

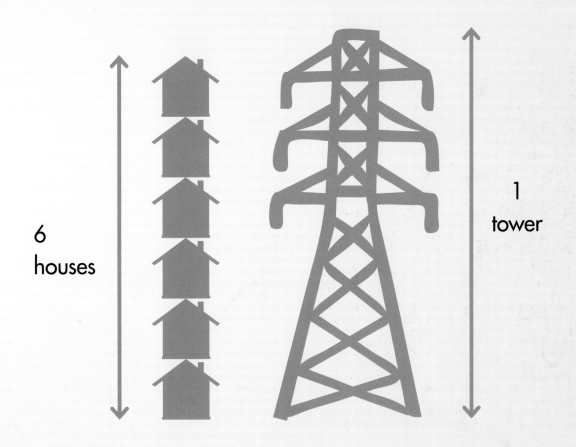

6 houses

1 tower

What is taller than an electrical tower? →

Wind Turbines

A wind turbine is taller than an **electrical tower**. Wind turbines are like giant windmills. They use the power of the wind to make **electricity**.

A group of wind turbines is called a wind farm.

A wind turbine can be around 295 feet tall. This is nearly as high as two electrical towers on top of each other.

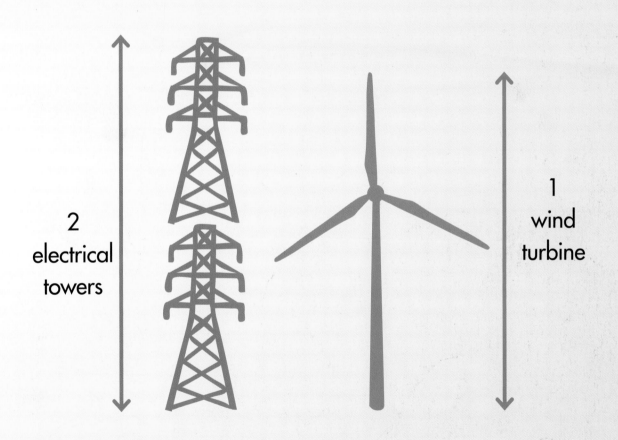

2 electrical towers

1 wind turbine

What is taller than a wind turbine? ➡

The London Eye

Fun rides such as **roller coasters** and **Ferris wheels** can be taller than a **wind turbine**. This giant Ferris wheel is the London Eye in London, England.

The London Eye can carry 800 people at once.

The London Eye moves slowly, so people inside the **capsules** can admire the view over the city. It is 443 feet tall. This is as tall as one and a half wind turbines.

1½ wind turbines

1 London Eye

What is taller than the London Eye? →

The Golden Gate Bridge

The Golden Gate Bridge is taller than the London Eye. The Golden Gate Bridge is in San Francisco Bay, in California.

Every day, about 107,000 **vehicles** cross the Golden Gate Bridge.

The towers on the Golden Gate Bridge rise 745 feet above the water. If you put one and a half London Eyes on top of each other, the Golden Gate Bridge would still be taller!

1½ London Eyes

1 Golden Gate Bridge

What is taller than the Golden Gate Bridge? ➡

The Eiffel Tower

The Eiffel Tower is taller than the Golden Gate Bridge. The Eiffel Tower is in Paris, in France. It was built to look impressive and to let people sightsee over the city.

The Eiffel Tower was built over 120 years ago.

The Eiffel Tower is 1,063 feet tall. If there were a **wind turbine** on top of the Golden Gate Bridge, the Eiffel Tower would still be taller!

1 wind turbine

1 Golden Gate Bridge

1 Eiffel Tower

What is taller than the Eiffel Tower? →

The Willis Tower

A **skyscraper** called the Willis Tower is taller than the Eiffel Tower. The Willis Tower is in Chicago, Illinois. The Willis Tower is full of offices. **Radio** and **television signals** are also sent from the tower.

The Willis Tower used to be known as the Sears Tower.

When it was built in 1973, the Willis Tower was the tallest skyscraper in the world. It is 1,450 feet tall. This is nearly one and a half times as tall as the Eiffel Tower.

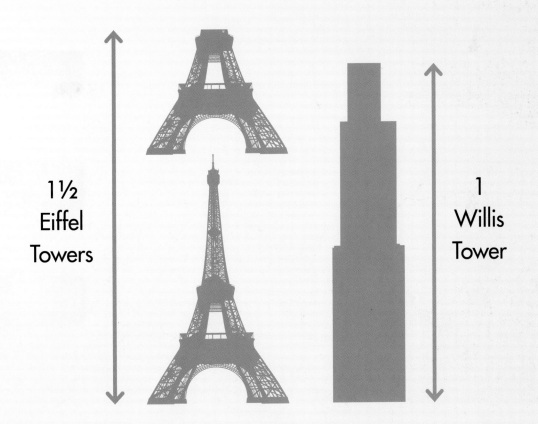

1½
Eiffel
Towers

1
Willis
Tower

What is taller than the Willis Tower? ➡

The KVLY-TV Mast

The KVLY-TV **mast** is taller than the Willis Tower. The mast is in the state of North Dakota. It is used by a television channel to send **television signals**.

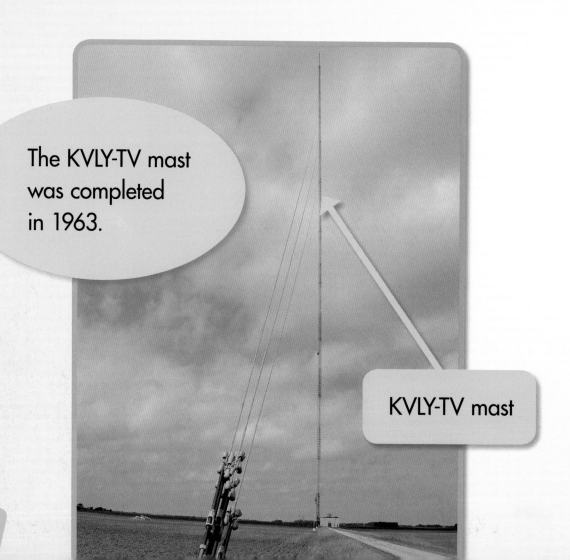

The KVLY-TV mast was completed in 1963.

KVLY-TV mast

The KVLY-TV mast is 2,064 feet tall. This means that if you put the London Eye on top of the Willis Tower, the KVLY-TV mast would still be taller!

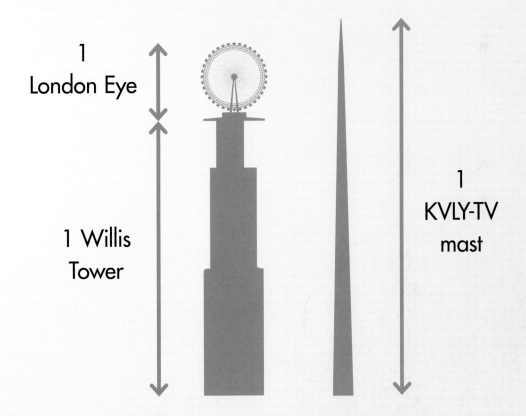

1
London Eye

1 Willis
Tower

1
KVLY-TV
mast

What is taller than the KVLY-TV mast? ➡

The World's Tallest Structure

Burj Khalifa is taller than the KVLY-TV **mast**. This **skyscraper** is in Dubai, in the Middle East. It is full of offices, apartments, and hotels. Burj Khalifa is the tallest structure in the whole world—so far.

Burj Khalifa's elevators are the world's fastest.

Burj Khalifa is 2,684 feet tall. This is far taller than the KVLY-TV mast. It would take you and about 704 of your friends, standing on each other's heads, to reach the top of Burj Khalifa!

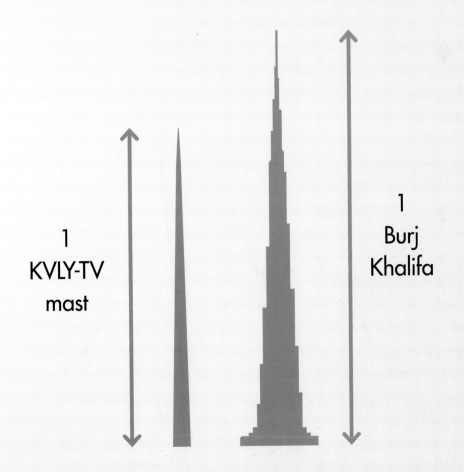

1
KVLY-TV
mast

1
Burj
Khalifa

Measuring Activity

Things you will need: rolls of toilet paper of the same size, building blocks of the same height, a tape measure, a pencil, and paper.

1. Measure the height of a door handle by stacking building blocks on top of each other. Write down how many are needed to reach the door handle.

② Measure the height of the door handle again by stacking toilet paper rolls on top of each other. Write down how many rolls this takes.

③ Measure the height of the door handle using a tape measure. Write down the height of the door handle in inches.

Find out: Does the door handle sound taller in building blocks, toilet paper rolls, or inches? Even though they sound different, all these measurements are showing the same height.

Tall Quiz and Facts

Remember

12 inches (in.) = 1 foot (ft.)

Very small heights are measured in inches (in.).
Larger heights are measured in feet (ft.).

Quiz

1. What unit would you use to measure the height of a doorknob?

   a) inches   b) feet

2. What unit would you use to measure the height of a lighthouse?

   a) inches   b) feet

3. What unit would you use to measure the height of a streetlight?

   a) inches   b) feet

Answers: 1 = a   2 = b   3 = b

28

Tall Facts

- Giraffes are the world's tallest land creatures. A giraffe can be more than 18 feet tall.

- A firefighter's ladder can be about 108 feet tall.

- The world's tallest lighthouse is the Yokohama lighthouse in Japan. It is 348 feet tall.

- Hyperion is the tallest tree in the world. It is a coast redwood tree growing in California. It is 377 feet tall.

- The world's tallest clock tower is at the NTT Docomo Yoyogi Building in Tokyo, Japan. It is 787 feet tall.

- The world's tallest **roller coaster** is Kingda Ka in New Jersey. It is nearly 456 feet tall.

Glossary

capsule egg-shaped compartment for carrying people

electrical tower large structure that carries electricity cables

electricity energy that people use to make lights, televisions, computers, and other machines work

Ferris wheel type of ride shaped like a huge wheel with places for people to sit while they are carried around

mast tall pole used to hold up a radio or television antenna

radio signal invisible wave that radio equipment can pick up and turn into sound

roller coaster type of ride in which people move along a twisting track at high speeds for fun

skyscraper extremely tall building for people to live or work in

surveyor person whose job it is to measure buildings and landscapes

television signal invisible wave that television equipment can pick up and turn into picture and sound

vehicle any type of transportation that carries people or things from place to place. Cars, bicycles, and trucks are all vehicles.

wind turbine structure shaped like a large windmill. Wind turbines use the power of the wind to make electricity.

Find Out More

Books

Oxlade, Chris. *Bridges*. (Building Amazing Structures).
Chicago: Heinemann Library, 2006.

Oxlade, Chris. *Skyscrapers*. (Building Amazing
Structures). Chicago: Heinemann Library, 2006.

Price, Sean. *The Story Behind Skyscrapers*. (True Stories)
Chicago: Heinemann Library, 2009.

Roza, Greg. *The Incredible Story of Skyscrapers*.
New York: PowerKids, 2004.

Web Sites

www.pbs.org/wgbh/buildingbig/skyscraper/

Find out fun facts about skyscrapers and try the
skyscraper challenge on this website.

http://skyscraperpage.com/
diagrams/?searchID=200

Visit this website to compare the tallest buildings
in the world!

Index